BE YOUR OWN

HERO

SENIOR LIVING DECISIONS
SIMPLIFIED

CATHERINE L. OWENS

Be Your Own Hero: *Senior Living Decisions Simplified*
By Catherine L. Owens

Copyright ©2014 by Catherine L. Owens

For further information about speaking engagements, professional consultation, special bulk pricing, or other related inquiries, see the author's website at catherinelowens.com.

Photography: Parker Austin
Cover Design: Cari Campbell Design
Interior Design: Fusion Creative Works
Primary Editor: Kim Foster

Print ISBN: 978-1-61206-076-7
eBook ISBN: 978-1-61206-077-4

Library of Congress Control Number: 2013950430

First Printing
Printed in the United States of America

Published by Aloha Publishing

DEDICATION

This book is dedicated to the seniors and families with whom I have been blessed to work with and have had the chance to befriend. I am deeply grateful for the lessons on life, love, hope, and trust that you have shared with me along the way, helping me become the person I am today.

To my daughter, Sabrianna:
May you always find the hero within you.

A HERO
IS AN ORDINARY INDIVIDUAL
WHO FINDS THE STRENGTH
TO PERSEVERE AND ENDURE
IN SPITE OF
OVERWHELMING OBSTACLES.

—CHRISTOPHER REEVE

TABLE OF CONTENTS

INTRODUCTION

Years ago, I helped a young woman move her grandmother into an assisted living community where I was working. Her grandmother had been recovering at a rehab center after a bad fall. She shared with me that they had befriended a man named Clyde, who needed assisted living as well, but had no family to help him look into it, nor could he physically come take a look at our community.

When I met Clyde, he was a frail elderly man who was completely bent over in his wheelchair, bitter and upset, reluctant to talk about his needs for assisted living. He wanted desperately to go home but had to face the reality that he could no longer take care of himself. He needed to be in a place where he could have his needs met. I worked with Clyde while he stayed at the rehab center. When he was discharged, he moved into our assisted living community and agreed to try it for a month.

Although Clyde was always grumpy, upset, and impatient with the staff, I had a soft spot for him. I often felt sorry for him because he had no family, had never been married or had children, and appeared to have had a sad life. Clyde was with us for three weeks before he passed away. I planned to attend his funeral because I didn't know if anyone would be there and I wanted him to have someone at his service.

I drove for over an hour to get there. I was running late and when I got there, I could not find any parking, which surprised me. I slipped into the church just as they were shutting the doors and was completely shocked to find standing room only for this angry, bitter man who I thought had no family or friends.

As I stood there and listened to his life story, I was speechless. Clyde had been a highly respected English professor who had shared his love of literature with a whole community. Former students, their parents, and fellow townsfolk stood in line to share how Clyde had helped shape their lives. Parents spoke of his gentle, caring, but strict nature that had helped save their troubled kids. Clyde had been a hero to so many people.

I left that day completely humbled and raw. I had felt sorry for this man because he had no family to care for him or to love him. I realized I had met Clyde, but I had never known Clyde. Who was I to judge what family is or what measured a successful life? Here was a man, who by most standards did not have much in terms of family or assets, yet had left his mark on the world and created a legacy that would continue to be shared and recognized for years to come.

It made me think about all of the Clydes I had missed out on knowing, because I had seen them for who and where they were at the moment I met them and not for the person they had once been or the life they had lived. I realized how often I, and so many others, miss out on knowing the Clydes of the world and miss out on giving them an opportunity to continue leaving their mark because of their age, lack of abilities, or illness.

Clyde had been a man full of passion and zest for life who had become angry, bitter, and hopeless. I didn't blame him, but it made me wonder at what point that had happened. That event shaped how I work with those in my care and how I train others to work with them. My goal is not just to see people, but to know them—know their joys, struggles, fears, passions, successes, and desires.

I have had the privilege of helping seniors and their families work through the difficult decision process involving questions about when to look into senior living options and how to go about it. What many don't realize until they are faced with this decision is that the process typically evokes many emotions for both the seniors and their families. The most common of these emotions are fear, guilt, denial, failure, loss of control or independence, and an overall sense of being overwhelmed.

In my profession, I meet seniors every day who still see themselves as young, still in the game of life, wearing their capes, heads held high, and ready to conquer the world. But I also meet the Clydes who have taken off their capes, lost their hope, and come to feel that life has nothing more to offer them—nor do they feel they have anything left to offer the world.

Be Your Own Hero is about facing the fears, struggles, and social stigmas that aging and health concerns can create for seniors and their families as they begin to look into senior living options. Deciding whether or not to move into a senior living community is said to be one of the hardest decisions a person will ever make. Understanding feelings about this type of move, personal perceptions of senior living communities, fears associated with aging, and how family dynamics have played a role in past decisions can help simplify this type of decision.

My hope is to help make it less stressful by understanding the emotional and physical aspects of this difficult and overwhelming decision and to recognize how, and in what circumstances, typical ways of thinking can create common misperceptions. I also hope to help make it easier to understand the many options available, to learn what services are provided, and to know what questions to ask when comparing services—but more importantly, to know how to ask the important questions.

INTRODUCTION

My goal is to help you make proactive, educated decisions rather than reactive, crisis-driven decisions, so you
may continue living a life full of opportunities and you
may continue to learn and grow, fully engaging with others, leaving your mark with all those whom you encounter
from day to day.

MAKING A DECISION

"You always have two choices, to accept things the way that they are or to have the courage to change them."

Jeckov Kanani

Accepted Thought Process: I will know when the time is right.

Reality: Uncertainty and emotions may keep you from making wise decisions.

Whether it's deciding where to go eat, where you'll go on vacation, or many other day-to-day options, there is usually some level of ambivalence in your decision. When making a decision to move into a senior living community, there is typically a very high level of ambivalence involved.

Feelings and concerns may push you towards making a change, yet underlying emotions and feelings may keep you from making a decision. An example is knowing that you need to make a change because you can no longer maintain your current home, yet struggling at the same time with the idea of leaving the home that you love.

For many, there is a great fear in giving up the home they have lived in for years. Many times it is not the house itself; it is what the home has represented to them. It may be the home where they have raised all of their children and built their life together. If it is the house that a spouse has passed away in, there may be a fear of leaving his or her presence felt there or the memories shared together in the home.

Many times, if you do not recognize the true ambivalence or conflict in the decision you're trying to make, it can be difficult to move forward. When this happens, it is common to state objections or reasons to not make a change that are easy to understand, such as, "I can't move until I sell my home," when really, you're having a hard time letting go of your home and all that it has meant to you. When this happens, it is easy to become stuck and put off making the decision you were considering.

Questions to ask yourself:

- What is the decision I am trying to make?
- What is pushing me to make this decision?
- What is keeping me from making this decision and why?

"Deciding to not make a decision" is probably the worst thing people can do, but it's the most common path chosen.

Notes for Concept 1:

MOTIVATING FACTORS

*"Promise me that you will not spend so much time
treading water and trying to keep your head above the
waves that you forget, truly forget,
how much you have always loved to swim."*
Tyler Knott Gregson

Accepted Thought Process: I'm just looking and researching my options.

Reality: There is something motivating you to look into senior living options.

Because most people wait until they are forced to look into senior living options—for example, living at home with in-home care, independent living, assisted living, or memory care—there is usually an event motivating them to look into such options. It may be lack of socialization and increased isolation, poor nutrition, safety concerns with driving, difficulty maintaining a home, medication management, dementia-related concerns and needs, or maybe just wanting the peace of mind of having someone there in case there's an emergency, such as a fall.

Even though the reason is usually related to something not working in the current situation, people often start the process of looking based on things such as community location, cost, apartment or home size, even the view in the apartment or the home. Although these things can all be important factors in the decision, they can take away the focus from the motivating factors prompting the inquiry. The most important starting point has to be based on what will address the motivation to look into senior living.

For example, if you feel that it may be time to find out more about senior living because it is no longer safe for you or a loved one to drive, you should ask questions regarding what degree of transportation support you need and what support each alternative provides.

When talking with senior living professionals about what services, amenities, and options they provide, it is important to be as honest and upfront with them as possible regarding what is prompting your call.

What is the first thing you say to a salesperson when they ask if they can help you?

"I'm just looking."

CONCEPT 2

This is one of the most common statements made when inquiring about senior living, even before the senior living professional has time to ask, "How can I help you today?"

Not only is it important for you to keep in mind the motivating factors when educating yourself on the differences in services, but it is also important for you to share with the senior living professionals the reasons for your call, so they can help answer your questions in the best possible way.

Questions to ask yourself:

- What has happened to make me feel like it's time to start looking into senior living options?
- What is it about my current situation that is not working?
- What will I gain by making a change?
- When do I think the perfect time is to make a change?
- What am I afraid I will lose if I make a move?
- What will I gain by waiting?

Clarifying and defining the motivating factors that are prompting you to look into senior living options will not only help you know what you are looking for, but will also help you narrow down where to look. Doing so can also help you recognize the questions you need to ask, and it makes the decision process much more defined and clear as you move forward.

Notes for Concept 2:

DEFINING INDEPENDENCE

"Facts do not cease to exist because they are ignored."
Aldous Huxley

Accepted Thought Process: As long as I'm living in my own home, I'm independent and in control.

Reality: If your home no longer works for you, it can take away your independence and control.

The most common misconception people have about moving to a senior living community is that they will lose their independence and control over decisions affecting them. People often equate living in their current home to remaining independent. This belief is often the greatest reason preventing people from moving into a senior living community.

Usually by the time someone inquires about senior living, there is something making the current situation challenging or concerning. Seniors are usually receiving some level of assistance that has made it possible for them to remain in their home up to this point. It may be help with things such as landscaping, housekeeping, transportation, or in-home care to assist with activities of daily living, such as bathing and dressing. It could also include an adult child or caregiver organizing and managing medications and assisting with meal preparation.

This can all be very helpful support and meet their needs on some level, but it often does not address the overall picture. Is it enough to address increased isolation, loneliness, and the lack of peer-to-peer interaction? If your current home or environment does not meet your needs or makes it difficult to manage those needs, it can begin to take away the independence that you are fighting so hard to maintain.

For example, if you are no longer comfortable driving, you may start limiting the activities and normal social engagements that you have always participated in. You may find it difficult to get to necessary appointments or shop for food and other needed supplies. You become *dependent* on others to help you do this, but it's at their convenience more often than at yours.

Sometimes making a move to a senior living community returns to you some independence and control in your day-to-day decisions. If you are currently dependent on family or friends, often waiting for their assistance, then you are not always in control of doing things on your terms. Maybe your meals are based on what someone will cook for you or bring to you. Your social interactions may only happen when someone is available to spend time with you or take you out. Trying to hold onto a false sense of control can trap you into a situation where you are completely dependent on others.

By waiting until there is a crisis to consider a possible move, you put yourself at risk of losing the independence and control that you are trying to hold onto because you are no longer making a decision on your terms. Making decisions under stress and in a crisis situation does not always allow you to make well-educated decisions and can often result in having to settle for the quickest, most available solution. It doesn't allow you the time you need to really understand your options and to make decisions based on what is important to you.

Questions to ask yourself:

- How do I define independence?
- What am I currently managing independently?
- What do I hope to gain by making a change?
- What am I getting assistance with?
- When do I think is the right time to make a move to a senior living community?

Shift your paradigm. Instead of thinking that you are going to lose your independence and control, take control of the decision while you're healthy and can independently do so.

When you are proactive and make the decision when you want to make it, before the crisis hits, you maintain full control of your decision. You are able to take the time to make an educated decision, to truly compare all of the different options, and to decide what you like or don't like about the different services available. You make the decision, have the control to do it on your terms, when and how you want, and are able to decide what exactly it is *that* you want.

By taking control and making this decision, you will be able to get things in place that will provide you with the level of support you need to address your concerns before they get worse or generate additional problems.

Notes for Concept 3:

UNDERSTANDING KEY INFLUENCERS

"People have a hard time letting go of their suffering, out of fear of the unknown, they prefer suffering that which is familiar."
Thich Nhat Hanh

Accepted Thought Process: I can't make the decision for my parents. It has to be their decision.

Reality: Your decision-making role may adjust, depending on need.

One of the biggest causes for stress or delay in making a needed move or change is not understanding who the key influencers are and their role in the decisions at hand. Their involvement is dependent on many factors and could change or need to adjust as the needs and situations change. Many factors can determine who the key influencers are.

- A parent or spouse may have Alzheimer's or another dementia-related disease and may not be capable of completely navigating or understanding all of the details involved in a decision of this magnitude.

- A spouse or family member may feel that it's his or her responsibility to care for the loved one, and this may keep the loved one from getting needed help.

- A widow or widower may not have been the key decision maker within the former couple, may not be used to making significant decisions without the input of the deceased spouse, or may be lost or overwhelmed at facing key decisions alone.

- The parents may be so overwhelmed by change and so afraid to leave what they know that they can't see how their current situation is negatively affecting their health, safety, and other needs.

- Family dynamics, whether good or bad, and how decisions have been made in the past can play a role in who will be the key influencers (see next section, The Adult Child).

No matter what details are contributing to who the key influencers are, the details of a move, along with fear of change and the unknown, are often so overwhelming that people would rather stay where they are, even if it's not the safest and easiest environment for them to manage.

It is critical to stay focused on the needs or concerns that are motivating a change. Most often the change needed will involve a difficult, seemingly overwhelming process, but choosing to do nothing does not address the concerns at hand. By choosing to do nothing, you are potentially setting yourself or a loved one up for additional future concerns or problems that possibly could be avoided by getting the necessary help.

The most common key influencer to decide if a move to a senior living community is the next step is the adult child.

The Adult Child

Adult children often play a significant role in this decision process, whether it's for a parent, aunt, uncle, or grandparent. They are generally the ones making the initial inquiry, wanting to be an active voice for their loved ones until they feel they have narrowed the options down to the best choices. It's normal to feel a need to watch out for their loved ones' best interests.

This can be a hard role reversal for the children because they're used to their parents being the decision makers and leaders in the family. Playing an active part in the decision, while trying to respect a loved one's dignity and independence, can be a tricky and very tough juggling act. Adult children often are the first ones to recognize the impact that a decline in health or ability to manage daily activities is having on a senior.

Adult children often have to be active partners in this decision-making process, hand in hand, side by side in the driver's seat with the seniors, helping them face their fears and the overwhelming details. It is important for the adult children to encourage and reassure the loved one that they are going to be there to help with every aspect of both the decision and the move.

When the senior has some level of dementia or other cognitive concerns, the senior's inability to process all of the details that are usually involved in making a decision so important to the senior's future adds significantly to the difficulties for all involved.

Think about where you are in your life and what it would involve to really make a move at this level—not to mention what would be involved if you were moving out of state, which a lot of seniors do to be closer to family. On top of the already stressful move, add the task of finding new doctors, changing addresses on all of your accounts, jumping through insurance hoops, and switching hair stylists, dry cleaners, banks, and so on, that you have used for years. For most of us, this would be very daunting and perhaps even overwhelming. Now, on top of all that, add aging, health concerns, newly developed personal limitations, and an overall decline in your energy and ability levels.

If seniors ask for help or move to a community where help and assistance can be provided, they may feel they're not doing their job and may experience strong feelings of guilt. Many spouses feel it's their responsibility to provide care for their loved ones. They need and want someone to step in and help them make this difficult decision. Their fear of change may be so great that, even though they know change may be the best thing for them, the prospect of it may overwhelm them. Seniors need their adult children to tell them that it's okay to make this decision, and they will have their support and help in the process.

The fact that a person is stuck due to fears or guilt or simply being overwhelmed does not alter or remove the needs and concerns that are driving the need for a decision in the first place. This is where it becomes so difficult to make a decision. Key influencers feel that their hands are tied, so nothing gets addressed. Unfortunately, there are and will be many times when the person with the need can't or won't make a needed decision. This doesn't mean it doesn't need to be made, but the most common reaction is for family members to not make any decision either because they cannot agree or because the decision is too difficult and painful for them or for the loved one.

Deciding not to do something is still a decision. It's just not always a good or safe decision. Many adult children have concerns for their parents' safety. Due to their parents' dementia or other health concerns, they are completely managing every other decision for their parents, but when it comes to this difficult decision, they put the responsibility of it back on the parents.

If children are sick, parents take them to the doctor. If they have a cavity, parents take them to the dentist to get it filled, regardless of how uncomfortable it is for them. It's probably a safe bet that the children do not want to go, they may be angry at their parents for making them go, and it may cause them some short-term discomfort. Regardless of all this, and no matter how much it hurts to see their children upset and in discomfort, parents do what they do because they love their children and know that a child's temporary distress can and often will eliminate future, and potentially more significant, pain and problems.

It's an act of love and care when a spouse, adult child, or family member gives the appropriate help and assistance that loved ones need, even if they don't agree that it's what they need or want.

Questions to ask yourself:

- Who is the primary decision maker?

- What decisions are being considered and why?

- Who are the key influencers?

- What decisions are they currently making or advocating and why?

- How have significant decisions been made in the past?

- If you have recently lost a spouse, what significant decisions have you made since their passing?

- How have current needs and situations changed how decisions are being made?

- How important is this decision to you?

- What do you feel is your degree of ability to make this decision?

- What will be easier about this decision if you wait to make a change?

- Do the needs go away because you put off making a decision?

- Is there a potential for the needs to increase or cause further concerns if you do nothing?

- If the current support you are receiving were to end, how long would you be safe living alone?

- What impact is the current situation or needs having on you, family members, and caregivers?

- When was the last time you felt peace of mind?

Elder Law Attorneys

An important step to consider is to meet with an elder law attorney to discuss and define your wishes before needs and concerns arise, so that you have the opportunity to document and make your wishes known. An elder law attorney's focus and expertise are on the needs and concerns of older and disabled persons.

Elder law attorneys deal with legal issues involving:

- Health and personal care planning, which include powers of attorney and living wills, lifetime planning, and family issues

- Fiduciary (financial) representation, financial planning, housing opportunities and financing, income, estate, and gift tax matters

- Planning for a healthy spouse when the other spouse requires long-term care, asset protection, public benefits such as Medicaid and insurance, veterans' benefits

- Capacity, guardianship, and guardianship avoidance

- Resident rights in long-term care facilities and nursing home claims

- Employment and retirement matters, age or disability discrimination, and grandparents' rights

- Will and trust planning, planning for minor or adult special-needs children, and probate

- Elder law encompasses all aspects of planning for aging, illness, and incapacity. The specialization requires a practitioner to be particularly sensitive to the legal issues impacting elder clients.

The following websites have useful information on elder law and include searchable directories of attorneys:

- **National Elder Law Foundation: www.nelf.org**

- **National Academy of Elder Law Attorneys (NAELA): www.naela.org**

Source: Area Agency on Aging of Pasco-Pinellas, Inc.

Addressing these concerns allow you, the decision maker, to make proactive decisions and to take control of who will play a role in making important decisions for you, should there come a time when you are no longer able to make them for yourself.

Notes for Concept 4:

ENGAGED LIVING

*"It's only when we truly know and understand that we
have a limited time on earth, and that we have
no way of knowing when our time is up,
we will then begin to live each day to the fullest,
as if it was the only one we had."*
Dr. Elizabeth Kübler-Ross

Accepted Thought Process: I'm not a social person, and I keep myself active.

Reality: Social interaction is vital to overall health and promotes engaged living.

Years ago, I had the pleasure of meeting Jack. My first thoughts of Jack as we began talking with each other were that he was a very confident, successful, and charming gentleman with a great sense of humor. Jack shared with me his sense of accomplishment as a successful, well-respected physician, his enjoyment of sailing, and the passion he had always had for it. As the conversation continued, he opened up a little more and shared with me that he had lost his sweetheart of fifty years a little over a year before our conversation.

There was sadness in his voice, but his eyes sparkled as he reminisced about the many adventures they had shared and the memories they had created over the years. He paused to take out a picture of her he kept with him. It was then that Jack became very quiet and a little choked up as he admitted that he missed her terribly. He also shared with me that he had recently enrolled in a continuing education class at a local college on "The Meaning of Life." He felt that he was lost and in a state of limbo, not quite sure of what his life ahead looked like.

Jack still lived in his own home and was, for the most part, managing his life *independently*, although he and his children had some concerns with falls. Jack was receiving some assistance with housekeeping and had meals brought in to help make things easier. He and his daughter initially inquired about senior living options because he was lonely. He stated that he was *active* and yet mentioned that he had literally spent the past year just sitting in his recliner, staring at the television. He was lonely, missed social interaction, and didn't like eating alone, but he didn't feel these were reasons to make a move into a senior living community.

As Jack and I continued to have regular visits with each other, he admitted that depression was starting to set in. He was not eating as well, and he was not motivated to get up and go anywhere. He continued to just sit in his recliner. He could see that he was slowly losing mobility, creating an even higher risk for falls. He found himself wondering, "Where is the joy in my life?"

Jack shared with me how lonely he was—how he really just wanted to be around people and have things to do. I reminded him why he met with me in the first place. I asked what his motivating reason was for making a change, as well as what he was doing to address the concerns he had.

I suggested Jack write down a list of pros and cons for staying in his home.

The following week, Jack and I met for lunch and he told me that he had made a list of pros and cons as I had suggested, but as he started to list them out side by side, he realized nothing on the list was as important as his overall concern and situation. He then shared with me his list. The sentence at the bottom was what he felt was the most important reason for making a change. The following is a copy of Jack's pros and cons list.

Jack's Pros and Cons List

Cons of moving to senior living community:

1. It's too expensive.
2. It would constrain a very comfortable budget.
3. I enjoy my current home.
4. I need more medical attention—best to consider apartment if more needs come.
5. I'm healthy now.
6. I have a marked concern about world events, including finances and their effect on Social Security and Medicare.
7. A move would increase the monthly draw on my retirement account by $2000 per month.

Pros of moving to senior living community:

1. It would be more prudent for my medical needs.
2. I like the new home there.
3. My meals would be provided.
4. Numerous experts are included.
5. I would have a much better social experience.
6. It would be more exciting contact with people (adventure).

"I no longer feel like my normal self. I feel withdrawn, timid, insecure, and very lonely. Having difficulty making decisions about this matter. I feel I must do something or lose my mind."

At the end of this exercise, Jack's statement at the bottom of his paper made him realize how critical it was to make a change in his current situation.

Jack had realized just how desperately he needed peer-to-peer interaction and companionship. He was at the point where he could no longer take one more day of life as it was. He shared with me that he had conversations with his deceased wife about the decision and change he needed to make, looking for approval to tell himself that it was okay to make the move and move on.

Jack left that day, told his children he was moving, listed his house, and began the process of moving into the senior living community. About a week before Jack moved in, I met with him to go over the final details and he was glowing. He stated that he no longer felt depressed; he felt hope for the first time and was so excited for this next chapter in his life.

Jack had been living in a senior living community for just a few months when he shared with me that he still missed his sweetheart, but he was not only enjoying his days again, he felt he was a part of something. He stated often what a difference it had made having something to look forward to every day and peers to share his days with. I saw a remarkable change in Jack as I watched him play pool with the guys, participate in the weekly golf scramble, attend the Veterans and Men's Club, and end each day at a dinner table filled with new friends and acquaintances, reminiscing of days gone by and anticipating the many days ahead and what they will bring.

Seniors often deal with loneliness, which can have a profound effect on their lives. They feel isolated from the world around them. It's easier to become depressed when feeling isolated, and this may affect their general health. It gets harder to get around if there's a lack of energy and motivation, while getting around less often leads to a loss of mobility. And what about the joy of living?

So many people think that the only reason to move into a senior living community is for medical reasons or when they can no longer take care of themselves. They often confuse *staying active* with being *socially engaged.* Jack is a perfect example of how loneliness and isolation can play a significant role in the decline of one's health, while staying active and socially engaged can benefit one's overall health and well-being. All of us at every age need peer-to-peer interaction. Throughout our day, we narrate the stories of our day to our loved ones—to our kids, spouse, partners, and friends.

It's no different for seniors. People often think because they have their kids, they have the social support and the emotional well-being that they need. However, all of us need to have peers we can talk with who have been through similar life experiences and have experienced similar successes, losses, decisions, and accomplishments. We need to interact with others who have lived through similar times and eras, and we need to just share day-to-day conversations with them. Peer relationships don't replace our relationships with adult children or spouses, but they are important at every stage of our lives and become increasingly important as we age.

Many seniors have the misconception that being socially involved means that they're just going to sit around playing bingo all day or they will have to do everything on a schedule. These same people, when asked what their current typical day consists of, admit that, aside from the activities of going to doctor's appointments, they're just sitting in their homes by themselves, doing nothing. *As much as we like our homes, our homes do not keep us company.*

More often than not, people do more in a community because in the community, they have transportation to and from activities, someone planning their activities, and peers to be active with. Yes, there are a lot of scheduled activities and events, but like everything, a person has the choice of whether to participate or not. For a lot of people, just having someone to share meals with allows for more opportunities to engage with others.

> Rex was a man who took pride in having open-minded and liberal views about philosophy and religion. He was worried that if he moved into a senior living community, he would have a hard time finding someone to discuss these views with.

I asked him, "Since you have a hard time getting out of your house, what are your chances of finding someone to discuss philosophy with?" He stated that the chances were pretty slim. I then asked him what he felt his odds were of finding someone to discuss philosophy with if he lived in a community of over two hundred people. Rex chuckled, as he admitted the odds were significantly higher. Needless to say, he moved in and, over the years, I have never seen him out in the community when he wasn't sitting with a group of friends, having conversations on some important topic.

Senior living is not meant to change who you are and what you enjoy. It's meant to add to and benefit your day-to-day life.

Questions to ask yourself:

- Who or what is your current social support?

- What are you currently doing to stay engaged with friends, family, or peers?

- When was the last time you enjoyed a day?

- If you are not doing the things you once enjoyed, what do you feel is keeping you from doing them?

- What do you think it would take to be able to do the things you enjoy?

Notes for Concept 5:

CALCULATING THE REAL COST

"I have come to the conclusion that caring for myself is not self-indulgent. Caring for myself is an act of survival."
Audre Lorde

Accepted Thought Process: I can't afford senior living, and it's cheaper to stay in my home.

Reality: Your cost is more than just dollars.

Cost is usually the first item that comes up when inquiring about senior living options, but it is not the only thing to be concerned with. A lot of people believe they can't afford to live in a senior living community. Most seniors have houses without mortgages and think that because they don't have a mortgage payment, their cost of living is a lot less than it would be in a senior living community. It is not realistic or accurate to consider "no mortgage payment" as comparable to a monthly average cost of $3,500 to live in a senior living community. If you were to sit down and itemize your monthly and yearly expenses, you would get a more realistic idea of what it costs to live in your home.

Separate from a mortgage payment are the costs of utilities, home repairs, property taxes, home owners' dues, food, and other additional necessities to maintain a home. Many times, there are additional expenses, such as housekeeping and landscaping, if you are no longer physically able to maintain the ongoing needs of the home. More often than not, the overall cost to stay in the home equals, if not exceeds, the cost of living in a senior living community. As your health declines, it can often cost significantly more to stay in your home, as more help is needed to make it safe and possible to do so.

In addition to the dollar amount of each option, it is important to consider both the tangible and intangible effects of staying in a situation that fails to meet your needs can have on your overall health and lifestyle. It is also important to consider both the tangible and intangible benefits of being in an environment that can support and address your current needs, needs upon which it is hard to put a dollar amount. Some of these needs are social and emotional well-being, the peace of mind of having twenty-four hour support, and the multiple benefits of fitness and wellness programs specifically designed for seniors to help them maintain an active and independent lifestyle. All of these things are critical to keeping people healthy and can often eliminate or lessen the potential costs of not maintaining good health.

These costs may be hard to put a dollar sign on, but being proactive and making decisions that may possibly prevent future health concerns can often prevent additional and unnecessary costs, not only to your health but also to your overall quality of life.

> Jane was a lady I worked with who was convinced that she didn't need to make a move because she didn't have significant medical needs and could still care for herself. She had a diagnosis of Parkinson's, which created some risk for falls, and she fell periodically. Moving to a senior living community wouldn't necessarily prevent future falls, but being in a home she didn't have to maintain, as well as being in a community that was more conducive to staying active, might prevent falls down the road. She would also gain peace of mind in knowing that if she did fall, there would be someone there to immediately assist her. She would also feel a greater sense of independence because she was no longer limiting her activities because of her fear of falling.

Another common worry for seniors preventing them from spending the money to get the services and support they need is the desire to leave money for their children. They don't want to spend what they consider to be their children's inheritance. It's important for adult children to remind them that it's okay, it's what they've saved and planned for, and it's important for them to have a good, safe, and enjoyable quality of life.

I often meet with people who have spent their lives being proactive planners, saving for a rainy day, yet they are unable to use it when the rainy day hits. For example, they will invest in long-term care insurance (which is one of the smartest things you can do) and continue to pay the monthly premiums, yet when the time comes for them to use it, they refuse.

When choosing a senior living community, people will often look for the cheapest option available, assuming the options all provide the same services, care, and amenities. *As with anything, you get what you pay for.* Although cost does play a significant role in the decision for most, it is important to understand the differences in amenities and services you are getting with the differences in cost. *Those differences often are what will determine your day-to-day satisfaction and quality of life.*

When buying a car, people will take the time to educate themselves on safety ratings, resale value, overall customer satisfaction, and personal comfort and needs. Most often, they will pay more for a car that meets a higher quality of standards because they will be driving it for years. Why not use the same approach and research state surveys, customer satisfaction, levels of staffing, and whether or not the community will meet your overall needs and desires that are important to you, when this is where you or a loved one will be living every day? Most communities provide the same basic services, but the level (how much they provide and staff for) and the quality of those services will differ from one community to another—all playing a factor in the overall cost.

Questions to ask yourself:

- What is motivating me to look into senior living options?

- What is important in my day-to-day life?

- What is important for me to have in a community?

- What are my current monthly and yearly living expenses?

- What is my monthly and yearly income?

- What assets or additional resources do I have that will contribute to my ability to cover my monthly costs of living?

- What value do I see in the intangibles I will gain by moving to a senior living community?

- What do I feel the cost to my overall health and quality of life will be if I don't make a change?

Annual Cost-of-Living Expenses Worksheet

Home Expenses

Annual mortgage or rent	$_____
Home owner's or renter's insurance	$_____
Natural gas or propane	$_____
Electricity	$_____
Water, sewer, garbage	$_____
Cable, Internet, phones	$_____
Housekeeping	$_____
Landscaping	$_____
Roof/gutter cleaning, replacement/repair	$_____
Carpet cleaning, repair	$_____
Appliance repair or maintenance	$_____
Additional interior/exterior maintenance	$_____
Propery taxes	$_____
Home owner's association fees	$_____
Other	$_____
Total annual home expenses	$_____

Additional Living Expenses

Groceries	$_____
Dining out or food delivery service	$_____
Household supplies	$_____
Newspapers, magazines	$_____
Entertainment	$_____
Clothing, laundry	$_____
Health club, other social memberships	$_____
Charitable contributions	$_____
Other	$_____
Total additional annual expenses	$_____

Health Care Expenses

Health insurance premiums $_____

Long-term care insurance premium $_____

Medicare Part B premium $_____

Prescription medications $_____

Copays and deductibles $_____

Other $_____

Total annual health care expenses $_____

Transportation Expenses

Car payment $_____

Auto insurance $_____

Gasoline $_____

Repairs $_____

Routine maintenance $_____

Transportation support if not driving $_____

Other $_____

Total annual transportation expenses $_____

Total annual expenses $_____

**Total average monthly expenses
(Total annual divided by 12)** $_____

**Average monthly cost of senior living,
not including additional care costs** $_____

What is typically included in the monthly cost of a senior living community:

- Rent
- Utilities
- Telephone
- Cable
- Renter's insurance
- Three meals a day
- Housekeeping
- Transportation
- Twenty-four-hour staff support
- Life enrichment activities
- Maintenance support

Intangibles that you can't put a cost value on:

- Social and emotional support
- Sense of community
- Peace of mind
- Safe and secure environment
- Opportunities to stay active
- Overall better health and quality of life

Instead of thinking that you can't afford to move into a senior living community, ask yourself: can I afford not to?

Notes for Concept 6:

UNDERSTANDING SENIOR LIVING OPTIONS AND SERVICES

*"Do something today that your future
self will thank you for."*
Unknown

Accepted Thought Process: Senior living services are only needed if I can no longer care for myself or a loved one.

Reality: Utilizing the appropriate service at the appropriate time will assist you to stay as active, healthy, and independent as possible.

Because the senior living industry is currently one of the fastest growing industries, there are new businesses and services becoming available all the time. Navigating the senior living industry can be overwhelming, and a lot of people don't know where to start looking or what services each option provides. It becomes particularly difficult when people wait to become educated in this regard until there is a crisis or some significant level of need for senior living services. Having established a substantial degree of understanding of the different options and the levels of services and care offered, can make the process of transitioning to senior living easier, more manageable, and less intimidating.

I cannot stress enough the importance of both seniors and adult children being proactive and educating themselves regarding the services and options available before the need arises, because both seniors and their adult children typically play a role in making this decision. Taking a reactive approach and waiting until you absolutely have to can cause you to make this very difficult decision during a highly stressful time.

Think of how difficult this decision would be for you at present. Now think of adding a health crisis or emergency to the equation and imagine how much more difficult and stressful it all could be. The main areas to become educated about are the different types of communities, the services and amenities they provide, what their limitations are, how they can meet one's needs, what will be paid for by insurance, and how other costs can be covered.

People often go through the process of educating themselves on the different services and communities, but they still make their decisions based on their fears, not their needs or what is motivating a decision.

For example, if you are no longer safe in your home because of declining health, yet your fear is of leaving your home, you may have a home care service come in so you can stay in your home. This may be the right solution at times, but if this decision is made to accommodate your fears and not your needs, it may only address some of the symptoms of your concerns and not the cause. The decision becomes a Band-Aid solution and doesn't necessarily stop the bleeding.

Although home health and home care can be a great added support, it's just a scheduled support. If you need support with ambulation or if you're at risk for falling, you can't always schedule when support is needed. How would your needs be met during the hours that you did not have support and care provided in the home? It would require hiring care providers twenty-four hours a day, which is not always cost effective and does not meet overall needs, including social well-being and staying physically active. Being aware of what the services provide, what their limitations are, and when it's appropriate to have them in place will be helpful in continuing to make proactive and safe decisions versus reactive, crisis-driven decisions.

Where to Start Looking

Deciding where to start looking into services can be overwhelmingly difficult. There are a lot of senior living referral resources that can be very helpful, but you should be aware that not every resource covers all of the available options.

For example, there are a lot of local and national referral agencies that advertise they will help you locate services and educate you on the different options in your area for free.

The most common way a referral agency operates is through the companies with which it has set up contracts. The senior living community or home care agency reimburses such agencies when a client they referred either moves in or uses their services. Although it may be free to you as the consumer, the referral agency may refer you only to companies where they have contracts, making it not always the best source for finding what best fits your needs and wants.

Many referral agencies just pass on your name and contact information to the contracted communities. They may not necessarily prequalify communities based on your financial status, your social desires, medical and physical needs, and other concerns you may have. This may cause you to spend a lot of wasted time calling and visiting communities that aren't going to meet your overall criteria. When choosing a referral agency, it is wise to use one that actually allows you to talk to a senior living specialist. Representatives should be asking you these questions:

- What is motivating your call?
- What types of services and support are you looking for?

- Are you prepared to answer income-qualifying questions?

- What is important to you in a community?

- What concerns do you have regarding senior living communities?

Such questions are good indications they are acting in your best interest and will refer you to the services and communities that will best fit your needs, wants, and other criteria, so you do not waste time with ones that don't.

Referral agencies can be a great place to start and their services can be helpful, but just keep in mind that you are still your best advocate. *You are the expert on you.* You know better than anyone the types of environment, people, amenities, and services that are going to align best with your overall personality, lifestyle, needs, wants, and values.

Based on the questions you have answered in the previous chapters, you should have clarified these issues:

- What is motivating you to look into senior living options and services?

- What is your available monthly budget?

- What do you hope to gain from this move?

- What additional support services do you need to add?

- What are your overall feelings and concerns in making this type of move or decision?

These questions and issues are some great starting points for you to keep in mind as you begin to look at the different senior living options available.

SENIOR LIVING SERVICES AND OPTIONS

Private Duty Home Care

Private duty home care is assistance with activities of daily living, such as bathing, dressing, meal preparation, shopping, housecleaning, and companionship, and is a private, out-of-pocket expense, but generally is included in long-term care insurance, depending on the policy and benefits that you choose.

Services

- Assistance with bathing, dressing, and personal care
- Medication reminders
- Housecleaning and laundry
- Errands and shopping
- Meal preparation
- Companionship

Benefits

- Provides added support
- Meets immediate needs

Disadvantages

- Scheduled support—needs and emergencies don't always happen on schedule
- Not cost effective if full-time care is needed
- Staff not always certified or trained to recognize or address serious medical concerns
- Staff lacks supervision while in the home
- Doesn't meet full spectrum of needs
- Lacks social peer-to-peer engagement

Average costs

Home care and home health agencies charge by the hour. The average hourly rate for home care is $26, with additional costs for overnight stays, weekend coverage, and second-person fees. The rate may be adjusted depending on the level of care needed. Someone who needs twenty-four-hour support to safely remain in his or her home is looking at an average cost of $10,000 to $15,000 per month.

Additional costs may include:

- Mileage
- Caregiver meals (must be provided if covering a twenty-four-hour shift)
- Holiday rates (usually billed at twice the normal rate)

Home Health Care
(Skilled Nursing and Physical Therapy)

Services

- Licensed professionals
- Assistance with skilled nursing needs (lab draws, medication management, and case management)
- Wound care
- Physical therapy
- Occupational therapy
- Social services
- Speech therapy

Benefits

- **Home health companies are licenced and overseen by the Department of Health and Welfare.**
- Licensed professionals
- Medicare will cover costs (with a physician's order) if care provided meets a skilled nursing need or if person is homebound
- Can be utilized to supplement assisted living where there is a skilled nursing need

Disadvantages

- Medicare sometimes deems need as a skilled intermittent need
- Doesn't meet the full spectrum of needs
- Lacks social peer-to-peer engagement

Average costs

Skilled nursing, on average, is $120 per hour with additional weekend and holiday rates. Physical therapy, on average, is $125 per hour with additional weekend and holiday rates. Some home health services are covered by Medicare if there is a physician's order for it.

Not only are private duty home care and home health care not always the most cost effective approaches to providing care, but they are not the most beneficial approaches to managing the overall social, emotional, and physical well-being of an individual. You end up paying a significant amount more than you would if you were living in a senior living community. Instead of a full team of professionals providing many services and amenities, you have one individual at your side providing assistance during scheduled hours of the day. Often, this can cause additional stress if the staff is not consistent and you have to constantly adjust to new people.

Many seniors state that although these services allowed them to stay in their home longer, they felt a significant loss of privacy when the caregiver was present, yet still lacked the comfort level of having someone there all the time. The reality is that in a senior living community, the staff is only there to assist when you need it, so they are not actually in your apartment or home unless you request or need their assistance. This can add to your continued feeling of independence.

Independent Living Communities

Services

- Staff members often available twenty-four hours (may vary by community)
- Light housekeeping
- Some or all meals
- Most forms of maintenance
- Social activities
- Transportation (may be included)

Benefits

- Someone usually available in the event of an emergency
- Safer and more manageable environment
- Maintenance-free living
- Transportation often provided, making it easier to participate in community events, as well as to manage errands and appointments
- Easier to stay active, helping to maintain physical mobility and health
- Social peer-to-peer encouragement and engagement

Disadvantages

- Care staff not on hand
- Staff not available to assist with activities of daily living or care needs

- Would still need to hire private duty care if needed
- Does not always ensure person's needs are met or available services are utilized

Average costs

The average cost for independent living is $2,000–$6,000 per month. This will vary due to many factors, which include:

- Geographical location—costs will vary by state
- Size and type of the home or apartment
- Location of the home or apartment. Rates will often be more expensive if apartment comes with a great view, has a patio or balcony, and is easily accessible from common areas within the community.

Additional costs may include

- Entrance or community fee, which is typically nonrefundable and can vary anywhere from $500 to $2,500 on average
- Second-person fee, averaging between $500 and $1,000 per month
- Parking
- Additional storage
- Guest meals
- Use of a guest apartment
- Activities requiring tickets or other expenses
- Hair salon and other services

Assisted Living Communities

Services

- Twenty-four-hour care staff
- Nurse oversight
- Assistance with activities of daily living
- Medication management
- Weekly housekeeping
- All meals provided
- Maintenance-free
- Social activities
- Transportation

Benefits

- **Assisted living companies are licensed and overseen by the Department of Health and Welfare**
- Licensed and trained staff members oversee daily needs and cares
- Care staff available in the event of an emergency
- Staff provides routine assessments
- Staff works in conjunction with senior's physician
- Assistance to maintain independence
- Peace of mind for senior and family
- Maintenance-free

- Transportation provided, making it easier to participate in community events, as well as managing errands and appointments

- Easier to stay active, helping to maintain physical mobility and health

- Social peer-to-peer encouragement and engagement

Disadvantages

- State regulations vary by state as to what care can be provided at what cost.

- Each company decides how their communities are staffed and how care is provided.

- Companies can vary widely on level of services and care.

Average costs

The average base rate (includes everything but care costs) for an assisted living community is $3,500 per month, and just as with independent living communities, will vary depending on several factors, which include:

- Geographic location—costs will vary per state

- Size and location of apartment

- Additional costs for care depending on level of care required and how the community charges for the care needs, averaging between $300 and $2,000 per month

Additional costs may include:

- Entrance or community fee, which is often nonre-fundable and can vary anywhere from $500 to $2,500 on average

- Second-person fee, averaging between $500 and $1,000 per month

- Guest meals

- Use of a guest apartment

- Activities requiring tickets or other expenses

- Hair salon and other services

Assisted living costs are private, out-of-pocket expenses, but generally are included with long-term care insurance, depending on the policy and benefits that you choose. Long-term care insurance will pay partially, but it depends on the benefit that was purchased as to how much it will cover. If you spend all of your assets for care, you can apply for Medicaid, which is state-funded support to cover the cost of care.

CONCEPT 7

Memory Care Communities

Services

- Secure environment
- Twenty-four-hour care staff
- Nurse oversight
- Assistance with activities of daily living
- Medication management
- Daily housekeeping
- All meals provided
- Social activities
- Transportation

Benefits

- **Memory care companies are licensed and surveyed by the Department of Health and Welfare**
- Secure and more manageable environment
- Environment often designed to accommodate dementia-related needs
- Situated near other residents who have the same needs, making it easier to have peer-to-peer interactions
- Staff is trained for dementia-related concerns and needs
- Staff provides routine assessments
- Staff works in conjunction with your physician

Disadvantages

- State regulations vary by state as to what care can be provided at what cost.

- Each company decides how their communities are staffed and how care is provided.

- Companies can vary widely on level of services and care.

- Not all communities provide the same level of training for staff on dementia-related needs.

Average costs

The average base rate (includes everything but care costs) for a memory care community is $4,500 per month, and just as with independent living and assisted living communities, will vary depending on several factors, which include:

- Geographic location—costs will vary by state

- Size and location of apartment

- Additional costs for care depending on level of care required and how the community charges for the care needs, averaging between $500 and $2,500 per month

Additional costs

- Entrance or community fee, which is often nonrefundable and can vary anywhere from $500 to $2,500 on average

- Second-person fee, averaging $1,000 per month
- Guest meals
- Hair salon and other services

Memory care costs are private, out-of-pocket expenses, but generally are included with long-term care insurance, depending on the policy and benefits chosen. Long-term care insurance will pay partially, but it depends on the benefit that was purchased as to how much it will cover. If you spend all of your assets for care, you can apply for Medicaid, which is state-funded support to cover the cost of care.

Skilled Nursing Communities

Services

- Twenty-four-hour nursing and care staff
- Physician oversight
- Can provide assistance with activities of daily living
- Medication management
- Daily housekeeping
- All meals provided
- Social activities

Benefits

- Can provide total care through end of life

Disadvantages

- Can be very expensive
- Typically not the most inviting environment
- Room usually shared and equivalent to a hospital room for cost effectiveness
- Food usually not very desirable
- Limited social activities

Average costs

A lot of people have the misconception that Medicare will pay for a skilled nursing community. Medicare will only pay for one hundred days per year *if* there is a qualifying hospital stay. A qualifying stay consists of a person staying three consecutive nights in a hospital and then being admitted to a skilled nursing community within thirty days from discharge to be treated for the same condition they were admitted for. If a person qualifies, then Medicare will pay 100 percent of the first twenty days and a portion of the remaining eighty days. Medicare also requires that the patient continue to progress or they will no longer continue to pay the remaining days.

After Medicare discharges the patient, a person pays privately. Skilled nursing communities charge a daily rate versus a monthly rate like independent or assisted living communities. The average daily rate for a skilled nursing community is over $200 dollars per day, with an average yearly cost of just over $71,000 dollars.

Long-term care insurance will pay partially, but the amount covered depends on the benefit that was purchased. If patients spend all of their assets for care, they can apply for Medicaid, which is state-funded support to cover the cost of care.

Hospice Care

Hospice is a type of palliative care, which is a form of treatment that does not attempt to cure an illness; rather, it is meant to relieve the symptoms that the illness is causing. Hospice is meant for those who are considered by their medical professionals to be at the end stages of life with a projected life expectancy of six months or less. Hospice's main purpose is to eliminate as much pain and discomfort as possible in one's final stages of life.

Services

- Emergency care available twenty-four hours a day
- Assistance with activities of daily living
- Physical therapy, although it is a limited service primarily intended to provide safety with needs such as transfers
- Access to therapists and counselors
- Pain management
- Grief counseling for families
- Oversight by a physician, nurse, social worker, chaplain, and many volunteers

Benefits

- Provides ability to maintain dignity
- Provides as pain-free and comfortable an environment as possible

- Emotional and spiritual support for patient and family members
- Can be provided in any setting

Disadvantages

- Deciding to choose end-of-life care can be a very emotional process for patients and their families.

Average costs

- Hospice care is covered through the Medicare hospice benefit, as well as through most private insurance companies.

The US Department of Veteran Affairs Aid and Attendance Benefit

The US Department of Veteran Affairs offers a benefit to war era veterans and their surviving spouses called Aid and Attendance. Many people are unaware of this tax-free benefit. This benefit is designed to provide financial assistance to help cover the cost of long-term care in the home, in an assisted living community, or in a skilled nursing community for those veterans and surviving spouses who require the regular attendance of another person or caregiver in at least two of the daily activities of living, such as bathing, dressing, eating, toileting, and transferring.

To learn more about this benefit, the qualifying criteria, and how to apply for the Aid and Attendance benefit, visit the US Department of Veterans Affairs at www.va.gov.

Be aware that there are many agencies, financial planners, and elder law services that offer assistance with applying and qualifying for these benefits, but many times there is some monetary gain for them. It is important to use an agency or person that is accredited by the US Department of Veterans Affairs to assist with this process to ensure they are acting in your best interest.

Notes for Concept 7:

MAKING AN INFORMED DECISION

"Education breeds confidence.
Confidence breeds hope.
Hope breeds peace."
Confucius

Accepted Thought Process: All senior living communities provide the same basic services and amenities.

Reality: What differentiates each community is *how* and at what level they provide those services. You get what you pay for.

When people inquire into senior living communities, cost is *almost always* the number one question. It *is* an important factor but shouldn't be *the* deciding factor. You can always get a cheaper room at Motel 6 than at the Marriott, but you also may compromise quality and amenities. Senior living communities are not apples to apples. Yes, most senior living communities provide the same basic services and amenities, but what differentiates one community from another is *how* they provide those services and amenities, *how much* of those services and amenities they provide, and at what level of quality they provide them.

The cheapest place is cutting something out somewhere.

In order for a community to charge lower rates, they have to cut overhead somewhere. The most common way to do this is to cut staff, which means they may have fewer staff members, each one trying to cover more responsibilities. It may cause the community to have fewer options with the level of amenities provided, such as with meals. There also may be less certainty as to who is responsible for carrying out those services and amenities. For example, who is preparing each meal? Is it a chef or a care provider, and how does that affect what type of food is served and how many options are available?

Cutting back on staff can also affect the community's ability to provide activities and programs and may mean that transportation or maintenance is provided less often. All of these things affect the residents' day-to-day quality of life.

Key decision makers often do a disservice to themselves and their loved ones by narrowing their selections entirely in accordance with the criteria of "lowest cost and closest location." Cost does play a significant role for most people, but touring as many communities as possible will help you to see and better understand what you are getting for your bottom dollar. Regarding location, consider that this is the place that you or your loved one will be spending every day of life. The food, services, staff, amenities, quality of care, and overall environment are what will contribute to your day-to-day satisfaction and quality of life, not the location.

Adult children often choose a location for their parents that is the most convenient for themselves, whether or not it is the best option for the parents. I cannot stress enough the importance of basing the decision primarily on what will best meet the overall needs of those who will be living in the community, since they will be the ones experiencing it on a day-to-day basis. The other common mistake I see is the senior choosing a less desirable community because it's in the town or city in which they have lived for years. Again, if it means going five miles, or even significantly more than five miles, out of your comfort zone to be in a place that will better provide for your needs and wants on a daily basis, such a place will most likely more than repay you for the extra distance you travel, both physically and psychologically.

Tips when touring senior living communities:

- Show up unannounced. Sometimes when scheduling a tour, communities have the time to put on their best show. You want to see what a typical day is like, not a planned and choreographed event.

- If you like a community, tour it several times at different times of the day, as well as different times of the week.

- Ask to stay for lunch or dinner. Test the food and the service. This is the food you will be eating every day, and food is one of the first things that will make or break your day-to-day satisfaction.

- Talk to other people currently living there and their family members as well, if possible. They are your best resource for how the experience will be for you. It is important to remember, though, that there are grumpy people everywhere who always have something to complain about. It is no different in senior living communities.

- Notice the degree of staff and resident engagement as you tour. This is critical. Do they know one another's names? Do they acknowledge and readily assist one another? Not only is this an indication of how your experience may turn out to be, but it may also be an indication of the level of staff turnover.

- Ask to speak both with the director or administrator and with managers of the different departments in which you have a particular interest. For example, if medication management is a high concern of yours, ask to speak with the person overseeing the staff managing the medications. He or she will be the one to best educate you on how and at what level the community will provide that service.

When you tour or call a community, the most important thing is not *what* you ask but *how* you ask it. Again, for the most part, all communities provide the same basic services. Your goal is to find out which one provides the highest quantity and quality of relevant services, based on your budget, wants, and needs.

Let's compare the difference between typical questions and questions that will draw out how the services and amenities are provided

Caregivers and Support Staff

A typical question is:

- What is your caregiver-to-resident ratio?

A misconception people often have is that a smaller community is better. With a more intimate approach, caregivers are going to know you or your loved one because there are not as many other residents there. Consider that it also means there is less staff handling more responsibilities. One community might have one caregiver to eight residents and others have one caregiver to twelve residents. Instead of assuming it's a better approach with the eight, ask what the caregivers' responsibilities are.

In a smaller community, caregivers often have a universal role. They're not only providing direct care, but they are also answering the phones after 5:00 p.m., preparing the meal, serving the meal, and maybe fulfilling additional responsibilities such as housekeeping. Although there are fewer residents per caregiver, the caregivers' roles are so stretched that the last thing they're able to do is provide quality care or even respond to the resident's call. When they do respond, all the other responsibilities they are trying to manage are set aside in order to do so.

The more informed approach would be to ask:

- What responsibilities do your care providers have in addition to providing care?

- What support staff do you have in addition to care providers (i.e., waitstaff, housekeepers, concierge, etc.)?

- What is your level of support staff at different times of the day, as well as on weekends?

- How many staff do you have providing overall support for the residents?

- What is your turnover rate?

For larger communities, you may have twenty-four-hour concierge service, so there will be someone to answer the phones at all times. You have dietary servers who serve the meals. You have chefs who prepare the meals. You have nurses on-site, housekeeping staff, life enrichment staff, and transportation staff. Although there may be a few more residents per caregiver than some of the smaller places, each caregiver's sole responsibility is being available to provide care, meaning you're going to get a quicker response time and more focused care. When there is a whole network of staff providing overall support, you are more likely to have a better day-to-day experience.

A gentleman named Henry lived in a smaller assisted living community that advertised, "A more personal approach." He was not satisfied with his overall care or experience, so he began looking into other available options. Henry inquired about the community I was working for, and I met with him at his place that evening to discuss his concerns and desires. We agreed that I would pick him up the following afternoon for a tour of the community at which I worked.

During the tour, he was surprised at the amount of staff on hand and the overall level of services and amenities. I tried to explain to Henry the differences and benefits of having sufficient levels of staff and the appropriate staff for each service, but it wasn't until I took him home that it became clear to him what the benefits were.

It was supper time when Henry and I got to his community. When we got inside, Henry told me that he needed to use the restroom. Henry was in a wheelchair and required a significant amount of assistance with this. When I told the caregiver, who was the only one on staff because it was after 5:00 p.m., she replied that Henry would have to wait until she was finished serving dinner.

I kindly replied that dinner could wait, Henry could not.

This is an example of how not having the appropriate staff can affect not only your day-to-day experience, but your overall dignity, safety, and well-being, not to mention that of the other residents as well.

Nursing

A typical question is:

- Do you have nursing coverage?

The only requirement by most state regulations for assisted living is to have nurse oversight. This may only include a contracted nurse who comes in every couple of weeks or once a month to check orders to make sure medication assistance was provided correctly and everything is in compliance with state regulations. If there is an emergency, the caregiver responds by calling a contracted, on-call nurse who may or may not know you or your loved one.

Some communities have their own nurses on staff to provide daily oversight, providing a more managed care approach. Not only can they respond to and immediately assess a concern, they know their residents' baseline and care concerns personally and individually. This allows for potential health concerns to be caught and addressed sooner. They may notice sooner that you're not eating normally, that your mobility or cognitive abilities are not what they normally are, or maybe that you are just not coming down to activities when you normally would. Knowing your baseline and when things are abnormal and being able to do nurse assessments immediately can often avoid trips to the emergency room, because they can call your doctors and generally get orders started right away. On the flip side, if you do have a concern that needs emergency attention, having the proper level of nursing oversight can be critical. Getting concerns addressed quickly or even immediately can make an important difference in the overall outcome.

The more informed approach would be to ask:

- What is the level of nurse oversight?

- How many hours per day and days per week is there a nurse in the community?

- Are your nurses employed by the community?

- What additional responsibilities does the nurse have; for example, is the nurse also the administrator?

- If the nurse is contracted, how often is he or she in the community, and what are the nurse's responsibilities?

Communities that staff full-time nursing coverage provide for a better managed care approach that will help to keep you healthier and independent longer. It will also allow for you to stay at the community longer as your care needs increase, minimizing the potential for you to have to move to a skilled nursing community later or at the end of life. *This may also play a significant role in the overall monthly cost difference between communities, but the difference in monthly costs may be far outweighed by the difference in potential long-term costs, both financially and to your overall health, when you either have or do not have the appropriate and added nursing coverage in the community.*

Meals

A typical question is:

- Are meals included?

Every community will provide two to three meals per day, but there's no regulation on who's cooking that meal, how many options are available, and what each meal consists of. In a smaller assisted living community, care providers may be cooking the meals and serving them. If so, it's often something that's quick and easy to prepare, such as canned soup or sandwiches.

The more informed approach would be to ask:

- Who is preparing the meal?

- Who is serving the meal? Are the care providers being pulled from the floor to serve the meal or is this function covered by dietary waitstaff?

- Are the meals preplanned meals from a food service vendor, and is everything out of a can, or are the meals planned and prepared by a chef?

- Are there multiple meal options? If yes, how many?

- Are the meals made with fresh fruits and vegetables versus frozen or canned?

- What is your flexibility with personal preferences?

Maintenance

A typical question is:

- Do you have maintenance staff on-site?

Most communities will advertise a maintenance-free lifestyle and provide some level of maintenance, but how many people they employ and what level of services they provide can vary greatly. Some communities might have one person covering multiple locations. Other communities could have each maintenance person covering one building, but the buildings might vary from twenty homes to two hundred homes.

If a company has many locations within an area, they may have one person to cover all of their communities. This doesn't seem that important, but it can make a huge difference in your day-to-day experience. If a community does not have the appropriate maintenance staff, they will be constantly dealing with emergencies and will not be available to assist with your individual wants or needs. This lack of availability will make it seem to you that you don't have a maintenance-free lifestyle.

For example, when a community has a good level of maintenance staff, they are available to assist with things such as hanging your pictures when you move in or changing a light bulb when it goes out. These may seem like little things, but it's generally the little things that mean the most.

The more informed approach would be to ask:

- How many maintenance personnel are on staff for your community?
- Are they responsible for more than one building?
- How many days per week are they on-site?
- How many hours per day are they on-site?
- What are the services that they will be able to assist me with?

Transportation

A typical question is:

- Do you provide scheduled transportation?

Most communities provide some level of transportation, but as with every amenity and service, it will vary between communities. A company may have one driver covering multiple communities where another might have multiple drivers covering one community. A person in a community with limited transportation may be picked up from a doctor's appointment after waiting for hours, while another person living in a community with a higher level of transportation staff may have a much better chance of being picked up immediately.

When transportation services are limited, it limits the availability for support, whether it's going to an appointment, shopping, or to events and activities out in the community at-large. Transportation services are critical to giving back a level of independence to a person who is no longer able to drive. Not having a sufficient level of transportation available can make a person feel a distinct loss of independence, because he or she is clearly dependent on someone else's schedule. In addition, a community that provides a higher level of transportation support will also be able to provide activities that keep residents engaged and participating in their surrounding community as a whole.

The more informed approach would be to ask:

- What is your level of transportation services?

- How many drivers do you have on-site?

- How many of your locations does each driver cover?

- How long is the typical wait time?

- What type of vans or buses do you have available? How many do you have?

- How many days a week do you provide transportation for medical appointments, as well as shopping and errands?

- For what types of activities do your transportation resources allow you to provide?

Life Enrichment and Activities

A typical question is:

- Do you provide regular activities?

Life enrichment and activities vary the greatest between communities, but they are critical components to achieving and maintaining overall wellness. Not only do communities vary on what activities are provided, but more importantly, they vary on the type of activities and the approach taken by the community when creating the types of activities.

"I don't want to sit around and play bingo all day."

or

"I don't want to sit around and do nothing all day."

These statements and concerns have less to do with bingo or doing nothing and more to do with the underlying fear so many have of losing their identity or being made to feel that they have nothing left to contribute or learn.

Every community will have some amount of activities, but not all communities will have activities that are considered *life enriching*. More important than knowing what activities or how many activities a community provides is understanding the community's approach and philosophy. Are they putting activities on a calendar to fill the day and keep people occupied? Or is the approach of the community to provide safe and continued opportunities for people to do the things they enjoy but were unable to do while living in their home? Are they providing activities that will provide residents with an opportunity to share their talents, knowledge, and lifelong experiences? Do they provide intergenerational activities and create opportunities for continued learning and growth?

When I ask people I work with what they enjoy doing, I often hear, "I used to . . ."

A lot of seniors don't stop participating in activities or hobbies because they no longer enjoy them. They stop because, often with aging or declined health, it may be difficult to continue doing the things safely that for so long brought them joy.

Betty loved to garden but was losing her mobility. With the difficulty of managing her garden and the unevenness of her yard, she felt it was safer to no longer try to plant her flower gardens, which for years brought her so much happiness. By the time Betty moved into the community, she was using an electric scooter to safely get around.

One day, Betty shared with the Life Enrichment Director her love of gardening and how much she missed doing it. The Life Enrichment Director quickly went to work to figure out a way that Betty could continue to safely enjoy her love of gardening and soon had whiskey barrel flower planters all over the community.

Betty was able to wheel right up to these and garden. It wasn't uncommon to see Betty riding around the community with her bag of gardening tools hanging from her chair, filling up an old jug with water and heading out to one of the whiskey barrel planters. Not only was Betty able to safely continue doing something that brought her so much joy, she was able to share her talents with others and feel a sense of purpose.

The more informed approach would be to ask:

- How many life enrichment staff do you have on hand?
- What is your company's approach to the type of activities provided?
- Do you have specific activities for the different levels of services that you provide (i.e., independent living, assisted living, or memory care)?
- Do you provide staff and training to address specific needs, such as mobility and dementia-related concerns?
- Do the residents participate in leading the activities, providing opportunities to share knowledge, experiences, and talents?
- Do you provide purpose-specific activities, such as intergenerational activities?

- What do you do if you do not have activities that meet particular residents' wants and needs?

This is one of the most difficult decisions that you will ever make, whether for yourself or a loved one. By taking a pro-active approach and educating yourself on the different services and options available and how each community provides them, you will have the greatest opportunity for making the best decision possible for you or your loved one.

Notes for Concept 8:

CONCLUSION

There are many social and personal stigmas and misconceived perceptions that are often associated with senior living communities and the quality of life they provide. Along with this is the misleading idea that independence in your later years is defined by staying in your own home, which often leads to avoiding discussing health issues, concerns, and options available to address those concerns until there is a crisis or emergency. Just because you avoid or ignore the need for these services until you absolutely need them does not mean the concerns go away. Avoidance will often exacerbate the needs and concerns, causing additional risk of further, often preventable, health problems.

I have seen many times over the years that not only the senior benefits from this type of a move, but the family as a whole. Spouses feel a sense of support and relief in knowing that their partners' needs will be met. Adult children have improved overall health because their stress levels and overall concerns are diminished, and they are able to juggle their own needs with their day-to-day jobs and families. As a whole, there is a greater peace of mind by all.

It is often said that education is power. I truly believe that by *Being Your Own Hero*, taking a proactive approach and educating yourself on the senior living services available should you need them, you will better address your needs and potentially avoid unnecessary health risks in the future. In addition, by being where your needs are safely met, you will continue to be able to live a life full of purpose, joy, and meaningful opportunities.

I DON'T WANT TO GET TO THE END OF MY LIFE AND FIND THAT I JUST LIVED THE LENGTH OF IT. I WANT TO HAVE LIVED THE WIDTH OF IT AS WELL.

-DIANE ACKERMAN

ACKNOWLEDGMENTS

My husband, Cliff—Thank you for your love, encouragement, and support through this project and everything else I aim for. May we always be helpmates, each to the other, as we both strive to grow and become better individuals and partners for each other. My love is yours, siempre.

My daughter, Sabrianna—Because of you, I truly understand unconditional love. Thank you for being the constant in my life and the happiest part of every day. I treasure the special friendship and connection we share. I love you and I am so proud of the amazing person you are!

My mother, Sylvia—Thank you for your constant example of compassion and service to your fellow man that has influenced so much of who I am and what I stand for.

My father, Les—I will always appreciate the "dark room" talks and the many times throughout my life when you told me how proud you were of me.

My "big" sis Angela—Your unconditional love, never-ending support, and friendship are gifts I will always cherish and hold dear.

My siblings Bob, Misty, Charles, Caroline, Angela, Joseph, Alan, and Jessica—For all that you add to my life as well as my family's life. I love the ability we have to always pick up where we left off and am thankful for what I share with each one of you.

Catie Kerns—Thank you for having the courage to *Be Your Own Hero* and follow your dreams and for the inspiration and motivation it created within me to do the same.

Victoriana Ireland—For all the "shut the door" conversations that have gotten me through the day. Your friendship, encouragement, and support are some of my most treasured blessings.

Gene—Thank you for your courage and willingness to share your experiences. They are sure to benefit and inspire so many others as they have me.

The Residents and families I share my days with—Thank you for the smiles, hugs, stories, and joys that you constantly share with me. My life is blessed and enriched because of you.

Maryanna Young—I am so grateful for the empowering encouragement that you give, so often just by the simplest of conversations. You not only make one believe anything is possible, you help so many achieve and enjoy all that is possible.

ACKNOWLEDGMENTS

The Aloha Publishing team—There aren't words to express the gratitude and appreciation I have for the role that each one of you has played in helping me to achieve this goal. Your constant motivation, support, friendship, and listening ear have been my anchor in this whole experience.

Brandon Wright—You truly exemplify the role of an ambassador in all that you do, and I will forever be thankful that you were an ambassador the day we met. Because of you, I was led to the person and team that I needed to help this vision come to light.

All the Aloha authors I have met along the way—Thank you for being a part of my journey and allowing me to be a part of yours.

Parker Austin—Thank you for the permission to use your "superboy" artwork for my cover design. The powerful message and the feelings this image evoked for me will surely resonate in much the same way with others.

Cliff Marks Jr. Photography—To some it may just be a headshot, but to me, you captured the essence of my spirit in a single picture. Thank you for sharing your gift and talent with me.

All the many friends, family, and professional peers I have not mentioned—Thank you for touching my life in so many ways and for the encouragement and support to always stand up and fight for what I believe in.

ABOUT THE AUTHOR

Catherine L. Owens is an advocate for the aging population and their families.

As a senior living expert, Catherine works with those who are going through the process of making difficult, life-changing decisions and transitions.

Knowing that these decisions can be emotional and often overwhelming, Catherine helps seniors and their families to understand and successfully navigate senior living options.

Catherine is well known for her gift of listening carefully to seniors and their family members, as well as to others, to identify underlying fears and concerns, helping them to find a real sense of purpose, and then encouraging them to live life to the fullest. Initiating what often becomes a deep and lasting friendship with individuals and families, Catherine's personal style exudes a sense of caring, an attitude of listening, and a dedication to, and passion for, serving others.

Catherine's compassion for seniors and their quality of life drives her to provide resources to the families of seniors, as well as to function as a continuing support. Her knowledge and her experience of providing for seniors' needs have given her insight and discernment, bringing into focus approaches that produce successful results for seniors.

Catherine's remarkable success and in-depth experience in Sales, Marketing, Leadership, and Training in the senior living industry have proven to be significant assets for her clients and their families, community leaders, and other professionals in her field.

Outside of senior advocacy, she enjoys spending time with her husband, Cliff, and her wonderful daughter, Sabrianna, and can usually be found either on the golf course or fishing near her home in Idaho.

THANK YOU

I appreciate you taking the time to read *Be Your Own Hero* and hope that it has not only been an enjoyable experience, but an insightful one as well. My sincere desire is that this book will offer some guidance, direction, and peace of mind as you contemplate and navigate the difficult decision of senior living services for yourself or a loved one.

If you feel that *Be Your Own Hero* has been a help or could be a resource for others, I would love to hear from you and have you share your thoughts, stories, or feedback. I can be reached at Catherine@catherinelowens.com.

Also, I would encourage you to write a customer review for *Be Your Own Hero* on Amazon.com. This is a great help to those searching for resources on this topic that so many are faced with, yet so often is not talked about. To do so, just go to Amazon.com, search for *Be Your Own Hero* by Catherine L. Owens and click on *Write a Customer Review*.

If you would like to stay current with updates on *Be Your Own Hero*, you can:

- Visit my website at catherinelowens.com
- Visit and LIKE my Facebook page at https://www.facebook.com/beyourownheroclowens

Thank you!
Catherine L. Owens